CW00501570

© International Music Publications Ltd
First published in 1992 by International Music Publications Ltd
International Music Publications Ltd is a Faber Music company
Bloomsbury House 74–77 Great Russell Street London WC1B 3DA
Arranged by Stephen Clark
Edited by Peter Foss
Cover design by Ian Barratt
Printed in England by Caligraving Ltd
All rights reserved

ISBN10: 0-571-52653-5
EAN13: 978-0-571-52653-6

To buy Faber Music publications or to find out about the full range of titles available,
please contact your local music retailer or Faber Music sales enquiries:

Faber Music Ltd, Burnt Mill, Elizabeth Way, Harlow, CM20 2HX England
Tel: +44(0)1279 82 89 82    Fax: +44(0)1279 82 89 83
sales@fabermusic.com   fabermusic.com

# Medley 1 - Quickstep

### AVALON

Words by AL JOLSON and BUDDY De SYLVA
Music by VINCENT ROSE

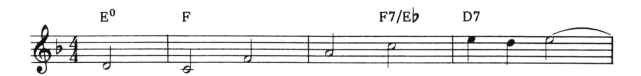

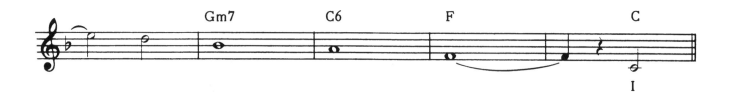

found my love in A - va - lon ———— Be -

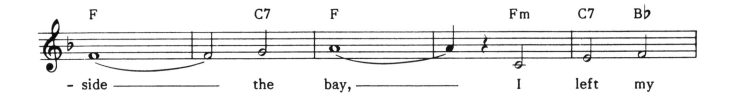

- side ———— the bay, ———— I left my

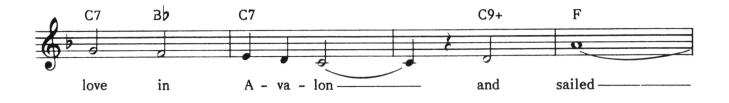

love in A - va - lon ———— and sailed ————

—— a - way; ———— I dream of

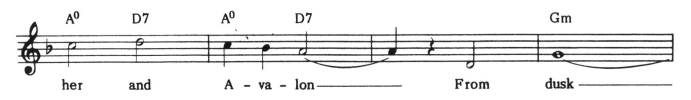

her and A - va - lon ———— From dusk ————

— 'til dawn, And so I

think I'll tra-vel on To A - va -

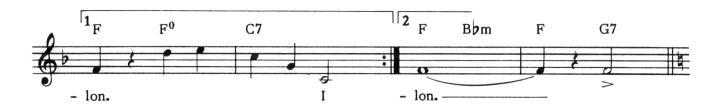

- lon. I - lon.

## ALL I DO IS DREAM OF YOU

Words by ARTHUR FREED
Music by NACIO HERB BROWN

All I do is dream of you the whole night through, —

With the dawn, I still go on and dream of you. — You're

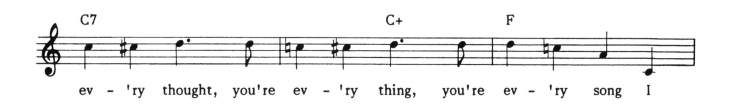

ev - 'ry thought, you're ev - 'ry thing, you're ev - 'ry song I

ev - er sing Sum - mer, win - ter, au - tumn and

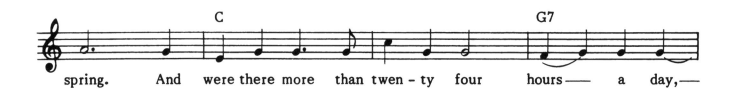

spring. And were there more than twen-ty four hours — a day, —

— They'd be spent in sweet con-tent dream-ing a - way. —

— When skies are grey, when skies are blue, Morn-ing noon and

night time too, All I do the whole day through, is

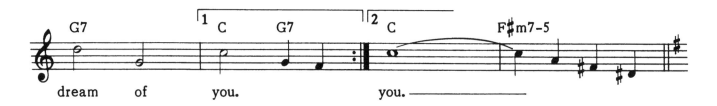

dream of you. you. —

## SWEET GEORGIA BROWN

Words and Music by
BEN BERNIE, KENNETH CASEY and MACEO PINKARD

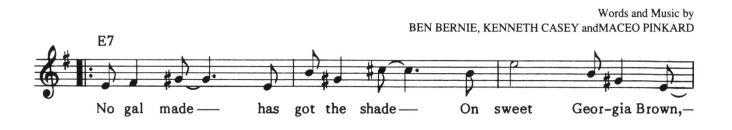

No gal made — has got the shade — On sweet Geor-gia Brown, —

— Two left feet, — but, oh! so neat — has

# I WANT TO BE HAPPY

Words by IRVING CAESAR
Music by VINCENT YOUMANS

# Medley 2 - Waltz

## LOVELY LADY

Words by TED KOEHLER
Music by JIMMY McHUGH

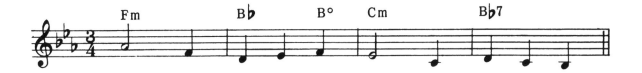

Love - ly la-dy I'm fall - ing mad-ly in love

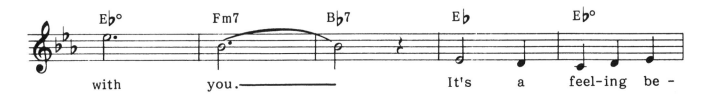

with you. It's a feel-ing be -

yond con - ceal - ing, What can I do?

— Take my heart it's yours a -

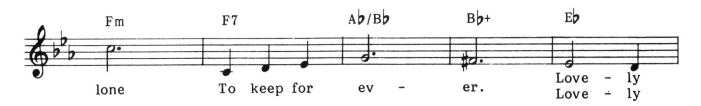

lone To keep for ev - er. Love - ly
Love - ly

la - dy I'm fall - ing mad - ly in love
la - dy why don't you tell me you love

with you.
me too? I'm in

# DIANE

Words and Music by ERNO RAPEE and LEW POLLACK

# MAY EACH DAY

Words by MORT GREEN
Music by GEORGE WYLE

# WONDERFUL ONE

Words by DOROTHY TERRISS
Music by PAUL WHITEMAN & FERDE GROFE
Adapted from a theme by MARSHALL NEILAN

# Medley 3 - Foxtrot

## I'M IN THE MOOD FOR LOVE

Words & Music by JIMMY McHUGH & DOROTHY FIELDS

# FOR ALL WE KNOW

Words by SAM M LEWIS
Music by J FRED COOTS

# MEMORIES OF YOU

Words by ANDY RAZAF
Music by EUBIE BLAKE

Walk-ing skies    at sun-rise,    Ev-'ry sun-set    too,

Seems to    be    bring-ing me    Mem - o - ries of    you;

Here and there,    ev - 'ry-where,    Scenes that we once    knew,

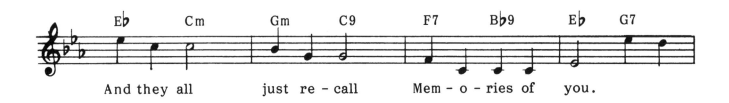

And they all    just re - call    Mem - o - ries of    you.

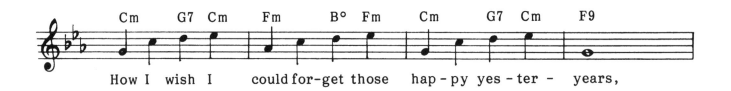

How I wish I    could for-get those    hap-py yes - ter - years,

They have left a    ro-sa-ry of    tears.———    Your face beams

in my dreams, Spite of all I    do,    Ev - 'ry-thing

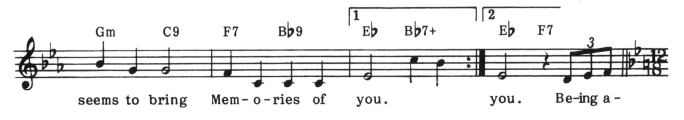

seems to bring Mem- o - ries of    you.    you. Be-ing a-

# JULIE, DO YA LOVE ME?

Words and Music by TOM BAHLER

-lone at night— makes me sad girl,— Yeah it
so much fun— to - geth-er — and I was

brings me down— al - right.————
sure that you — were mine.———— But

Toss - in' and turn - in' and freez - in' and burn-in' and
leav - in' you ba - by is driv -in' me cra - zy it's

cry - in'— all through——— the night. Yeah.———
got me— won-d'ring——— all the time. Yeah.———

Jul -ie, Jul - ie, Jul - ie, do ya love ——— me? ———

Jul -ie, Jul-ie, Jul-ie, do you care?— Jul- ie, Jul - ie are you think-ing of—

— me? — Jul -ie, Jul -ie will you still- be there?

We had there? ———

# Medley 4 - Quickstep

## WHISPERING

Words by JOHN SCHONBERGER
Music by MALVIN SCHONBERGER

# THERE'S A RAINBOW 'ROUND MY SHOULDER

Words and Music by AL JOLSON,
BILLY ROSE and DAVE DREYER

# THREE LITTLE WORDS

Words by BERT KALMAR
Music by HARRY RUBY

Three lit - tle words, _____ Oh, what I'd give for that

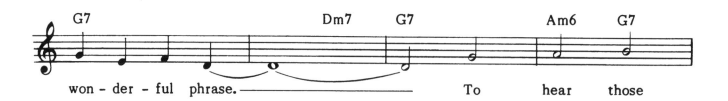

won - der - ful phrase. _____ To hear those

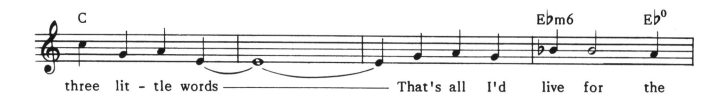

three lit - tle words _____ That's all I'd live for the

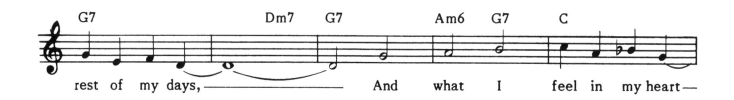

rest of my days, _____ And what I feel in my heart _____

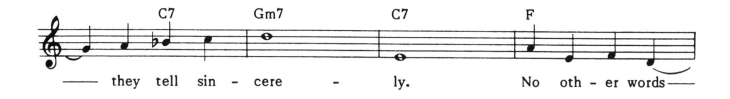

_____ they tell sin - cere - ly. No oth - er words _____

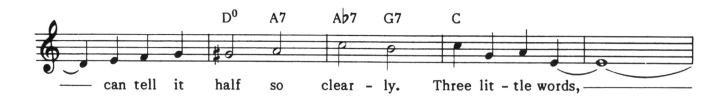

_____ can tell it half so clear - ly. Three lit - tle words, _____

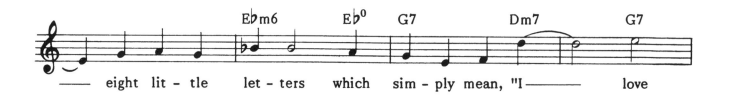

_____ eight lit - tle let - ters which sim - ply mean, "I _____ love

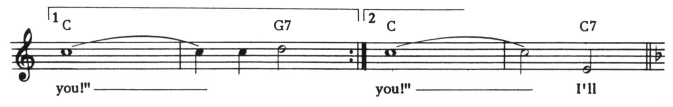

you!" _____       you!" _____       I'll

# I'LL SEE YOU IN MY DREAMS

Words by GUS KAHN
Music by ISHAM JONES

Bb                                   Bbm6

see      you      in      my      dreams, ————

F                    F0      E7      F6

Hold     you      in      my      dreams, ————

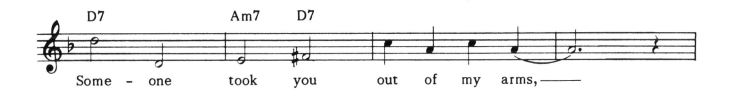

D7                    Am7      D7

Some - one      took      you      out      of      my      arms, ————

G7                    G6      G7      C7

Still      I      feel      the      thrill      of      your      charms. ————

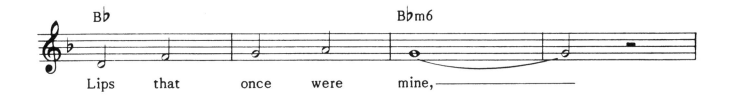

Bb                                   Bbm6

Lips      that      once      were      mine, ————

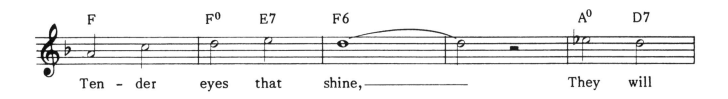

F                    F0      E7      F6                    A0      D7

Ten - der      eyes      that      shine, ————                    They      will

A7                    Dm      Am7      Bb      Bbm6      C7

light      my      way      to - night,      I'll      see      you      in      my

1. F          Bbm6      C7          2. F      Bbm6      F

dreams. ————            I'll      dreams. ————

# Medley 5 - Waltz

## THREE O'CLOCK IN THE MORNING

Words by DOROTHY TERRISS
Music by JULIAN ROBLEDO

Clock strikes

It's three o' - clock in the morn - ing, We've

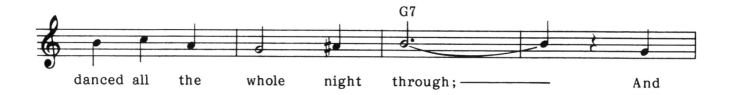

danced all the whole night through; —————— And

day - light soon will be dawn - ing,

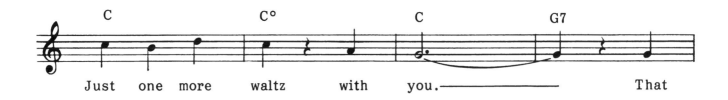

Just one more waltz with you.————— That

mel - o - dy so en - tranc - ing,

Seems to be made for us two, —————

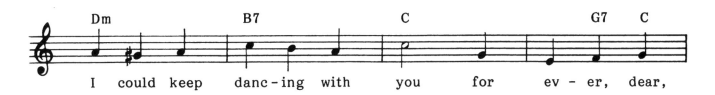

I could keep danc-ing with you for ev-er, dear,

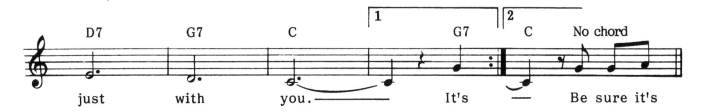

just with you. It's Be sure it's

## IT'S A SIN TO TELL A LIE

Words and Music by BILLY MAYHEW

true when you say "I love you," It's a

sin to tell a lie.

Mil - lions of hearts have been bro - ken,

Just be-cause these words were spo -

ken. I love you, yes, I do, I love

you, If you break my heart I'll die.— So be sure it's true, When you say "I love you," It's a sin to tell a lie.— Be sure it's

## FOR YOU

Words by AL DUBIN
Music by JOE BURKE

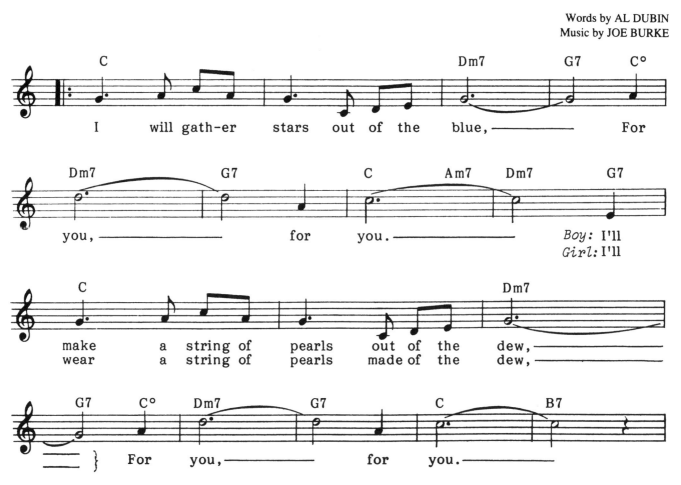

I will gath-er stars out of the blue,— For you,— for you.— *Boy:* I'll *Girl:* I'll make a string of pearls out of the dew,— wear a string of pearls made of the dew,— For you,— for you.—

## IN A SHANTY IN OLD SHANTY TOWN

Words by JOE YOUNG
Music by LITTLE JACK LITTLE and JOHN SIRAS

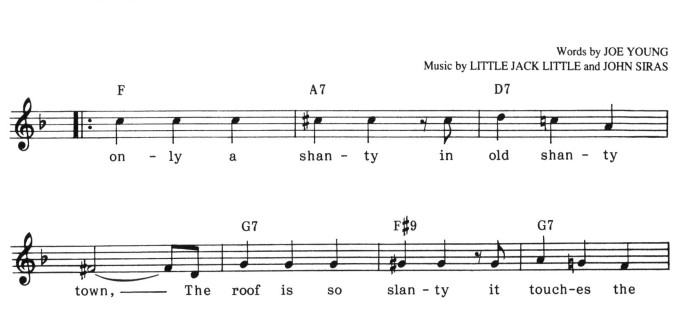

24

# Medley 6 - Foxtrot

## ONCE IN A WHILE

Words by BUD GREEN
Music by MICHAEL EDWARDS

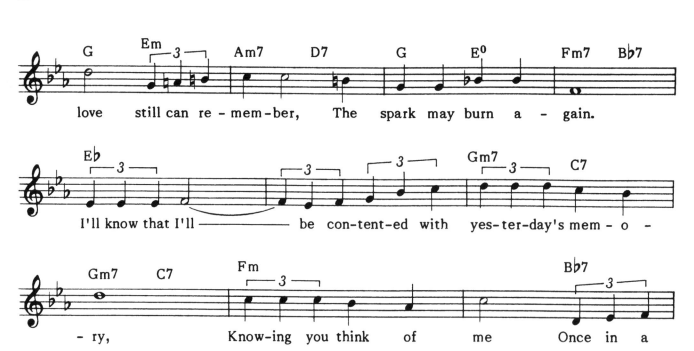

love still can re-mem-ber, The spark may burn a-gain.

I'll know that I'll — be con-tent-ed with yes-ter-day's mem-o-

-ry, Know-ing you think of me Once in a

while. while.

## WHEN I FALL IN LOVE

Words by EDWARD HEYMAN
Music by VICTOR YOUNG

When I fall in love it will be for-ev-er,

Or I'll nev-er fall in love. — In a

rest-less world like this is, love is end-ed be-fore it's be-

-gun, And too man-y moon-light kiss-es seem to

cool in the warmth of the sun. When I give my heart

it will be com - plete - ly, or I'll nev - er give my

heart.———————— And the mo - ment I can feel that you

feel that way too, Is when I fall in love with

you.———————— you.————————

## WHEN YOU WISH UPON A STAR

Words by NED WASHINGTON
Music by LEIGH HARLINE

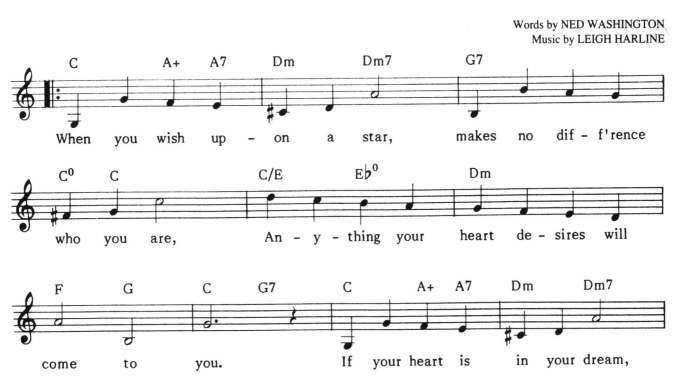

When you wish up - on a star, makes no dif - f'rence

who you are, An - y - thing your heart de - sires will

come to you. If your heart is in your dream,

28

no re-quest is too ex-treme, When you wish up - on a star as
dream - ers do. Fate is kind, She brings to
those who love, the sweet ful - fill-ment of their se -cret
long - ing. Like a bolt out of the blue,
Fate steps in and sees you through When you wish up - on a star your
dream comes true. dream comes true. Blue

## BLUE MOON

Words by LORENZ HART
Music by RICHARD RODGERS

moon, you saw me stand-ing a - lone
With-out a dream in my heart With-out a love of my own.

© 1934 & 1992 EMI Robbins Catalog Inc., USA
EMI United Partnership Ltd. London WC2H OEA

# Medley 7 - Quickstep

## MY BLUE HEAVEN

Words by GEORGE WHITING
Music by WALTER DONALDSON

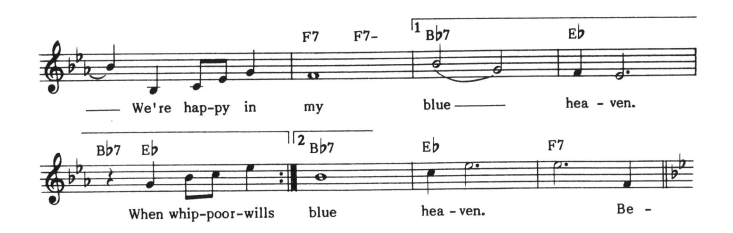

We're hap-py in my blue —— hea-ven.

When whip-poor-wills blue hea-ven. Be-

## BEYOND THE BLUE HORIZON

Words by LEO ROBIN
Music by RICHARD A WHITING & W FRANKIE HARLING

- yond the blue ho - riz - on,

Waits a beau - ti - ful day. —— Good -

- bye to things that bore me, Joy is

wait - ing for me. I see a

blue ho - riz - on, My life has

on - ly be - gun. —— Be - yond the

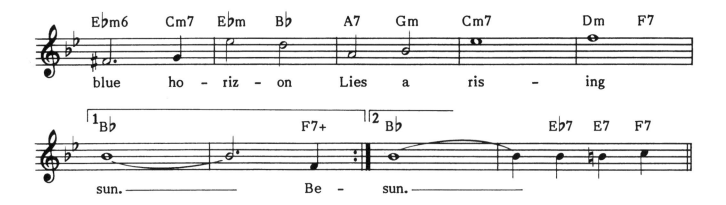

## BYE BYE BLUES

Words and Music by FRED HAMM, DAVE BENNETT,
BERT LOWN and CHAUNCEY GRAY

## ALL OF ME

Words and Music by SEYMOUR SIMONS
and GERALD MARKS

# Medley 8 - Waltz

## ALICE BLUE GOWN

Words by JOSEPH McCARTHY
Music by HARRY TIERNEY

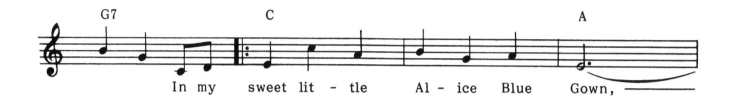

In my sweet lit - tle Al - ice Blue Gown,

When I first wan - dered down in to town,

I was both proud and shy, As I felt ev - 'ry

eye, But in ev - 'ry shop win - dow I'd primp, pass - ing

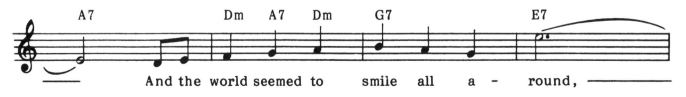

by. Then in man - ner of fash - ion I'd frown,

And the world seemed to smile all a - round,

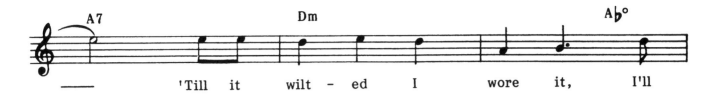

'Till it wilt - ed I wore it, I'll

al - ways a - dore it, My sweet lit - tle Al - ice Blue

Gown.    In my Gown.    A -

## AROUND THE WORLD

Words by HAROLD ADAMSON
Music by VICTOR YOUNG

- round    the    world    I    searched    for

you,    I    trav-elled    on    when hope was    gone    to    keep a

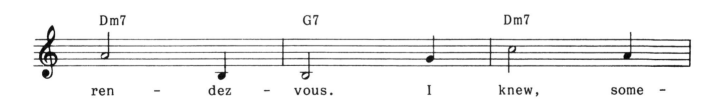

ren - dez - vous.    I    knew,    some -

where,    some - time,    some - how    you'd look at

## LET BY-GONES BE BY-GONES

Words & Music by JOS, GEO, GILBERT

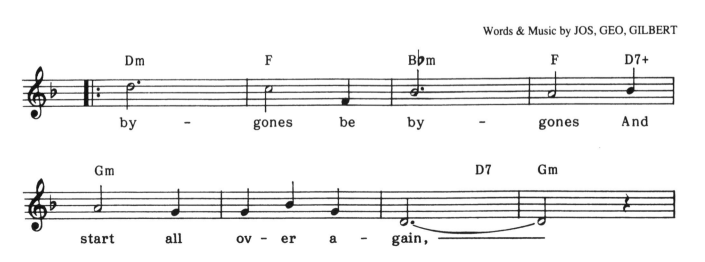

## PARADISE

Words by NACIO HERB BROWN and GORDON CLIFFORD
Music by NACIO HERB BROWN

38

# Medley 9 - Foxtrot

## RED ROSES FOR A BLUE LADY

Words & Music by SID TEPPER & ROY C BENNETT

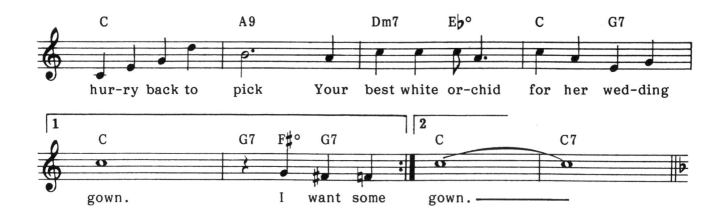

## JUST LOVING YOU

Words & Music by TOM SPRINGFIELD

## THE MORE I SEE YOU

Words by MACK GORDON
Music by HARRY WARREN

The more I see you ——— as years go by? ———

—— I know the on-ly one for me can on-ly be you. ——

My arms won't free you, ——— my heart won't

1.
try. ——————— The more I try.

2.
The more I try. Start spread-ing the

## THEME FROM NEW YORK, NEW YORK

Words by FRED EBB
Music by JOHN KANDER

news, I'm leav-ing to - day, I wan - na

be a part— of it New York, New York.

These vag-a-bond shoes are long-ing to stray,

And step a - round the heart—of it, New York, New York.

43

# Medley 10 - Quickstep

## JUST IN TIME

Words by BETTY COMDEN and ADOLPH GREEN
Music by JULE STYNE

Just in time — I found you just in time —

— Be - fore you came, my time — was run - ning low. —

— I was lost, — the los - ing dice were tossed —

— My brid - ges all were crossed, — no - where to

go. — Now you're here — and now I

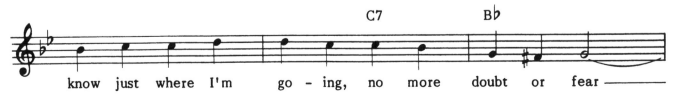

know just where I'm go - ing, no more doubt or fear —

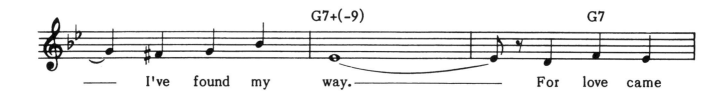

I've found my way. For love came

just in time. You found me just in time

and changed my lone-ly life, that love-ly

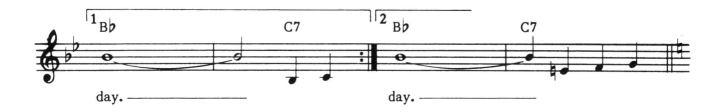

day. day.

## BYE BYE BLACKBIRD

Words by MORT DIXON
Music by RAY HENDERSON

Pack up all my care and woe, Here I go

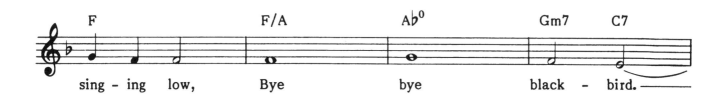

sing-ing low, Bye bye black-bird.

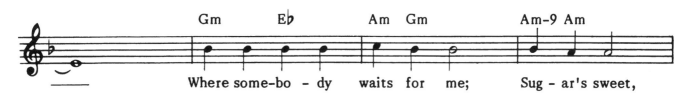

Where some-bo-dy waits for me; Sug-ar's sweet,

so is she, Bye bye black - bird.

No - one here can love and un - der - stand

me, Oh what hard luck stor - ies they all hand

me. Make my bed and light the light, I'll ar - rive

late to - night Black - bird, bye

bye. bye. I'm the

## THE SHEIK OF ARABY

Words by HARRY B SMITH and FRANCIS WHEELER
Music by TED SNYDER

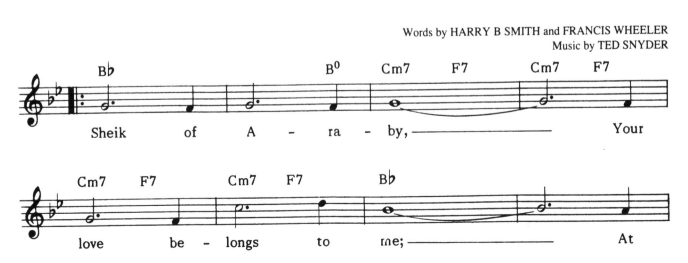

Sheik of A - ra - by, Your

love be - longs to me; At

night when you're a - sleep ——————— In -
- to your tent I'll creep. ——————— The
stars that shine a - bove, ——————— Will
light our way to love. ——————— You'll rule this
land with me, ——————— The Sheik of A - ra -
- by. ——————— I'm the - by. ——————— I've

## I'VE GOT YOU UNDER MY SKIN

Words and Music by COLE PORTER

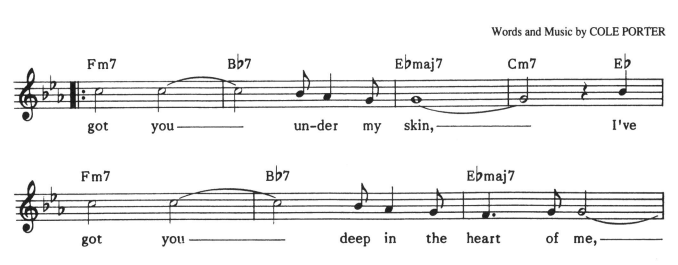

got you ——— un-der my skin, ——————— I've
got you ——— deep in the heart of me, ———————

# Medley 11 - Old Tyme Waltz

## TALES FROM THE VIENNA WOODS

Words and Music by Strauss

## SAY WONDERFUL THINGS

Words and Music by NORMAN NEWELL & PHILIP GREEN

Say won-der-ful things to me, I think you're
won-der-ful too. Say won-der-ful
things to me, E-spe-cial-ly I love you. They

say I was liv-ing — be-fore we met, All of my
more that I see you — the more it seems, Peo-ple should

yes-ter-days I for-get, Now you are the one that
al-ways be-lieve in dreams, Now all of my dreams I'm

I'm liv-ing for, And each day I love you more.
dream-ing of you, And some-day they'll all come true.

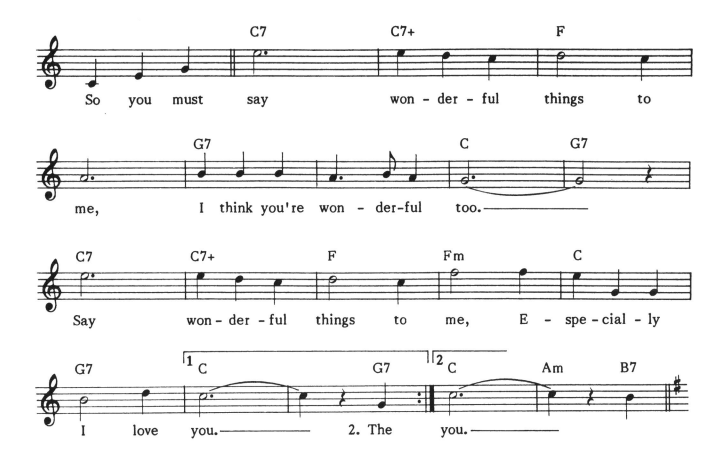

So you must say won-der-ful things to me, I think you're won-der-ful too. Say won-der-ful things to me, E-spe-cial-ly I love you. 2. The you.

## DELILAH

Words and Music by LES REED and BARRY MASON

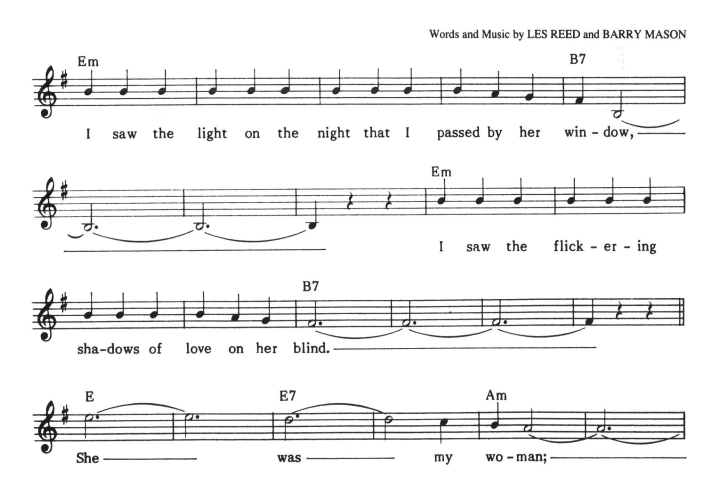

I saw the light on the night that I passed by her win-dow, I saw the flick-er-ing sha-dows of love on her blind. She was my wo-man;

52

# MY HEART CRIES FOR YOU

Words and Music by CARL SIGMAN and PERCY FAITH

# Medley 12 - Novelty Dance

## MARCH OF THE MODS
## (THE FINNJENKA DANCE)

Words and Music by TONY CARR

## LET'S TWIST AGAIN

Words and Music by KAL MANN & DAVE APPELL

twist a-gain— like we did last sum-mer,—

Yea, let's twist a-gain— like we did last year.—

Don't you re - mem-ber when

things were real-ly hum-ming,— Yea, let's

twist a-gain,— Twist-ing time is here. —

Ee - ah round 'n a round 'n-a up 'n down we go ——— a — gain; Oh ba-by make me know you love me so ——— an'——— then, Let's twist a-gain— like we did last sum-mer, —— Yea, let's twist a-gain,— like we did last year.-

1
Come on let's

2

## DOIN' THE SLOSH

by TONY CARR and ROY CARR

# Medley 13 - Roarin' Twenties

## YES SIR, THAT'S MY BABY

Words by GUS KAHN
Music by WALTER DONALDSON

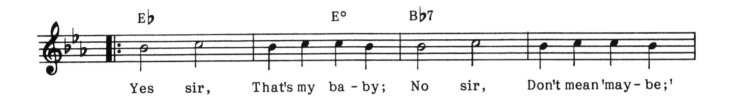

Yes sir, That's my ba-by; No sir, Don't mean 'may-be;'

Yes sir, That's my ba-by now.

Yes ma'am, we've de-cid-ed; No ma'am, we won't hide it;

Yes ma'am you're in-vit-ed now. By the Pret-ty

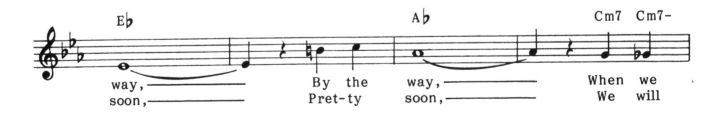

way, By the way, When we
soon, Pret-ty soon, We will

reach the preach-er I'll say
hear that Lo-hen-grin tune,

Yes sir, That's my ba - by; No sir,
Yes sir, She's for me sir; Who for,

don't mean 'may - be'
should she be, sir? } Yes sir, That's my ba - by

1
now.

2
now.

## AIN'T WE GOT FUN

Words by GUS KAHN & RAYMOND B EGAN
Music by RICHARD A WHITING

Ev - 'ry morn - ing, ev - 'ry eve - ning, Ain't we got

fun,
Not much mon - ey, Oh, but hon - ey,
Twins and cares, dear, come in pairs, dear,

Ain't we got fun. The rent's un - paid, dear,
Ain't we got fun. We've on - ly start - ed

We have-n't a sou, But smiles were
Our fam - i - ly tree, We're not down -

made, dear, For me and for you,
- heart - ed We might have had three,

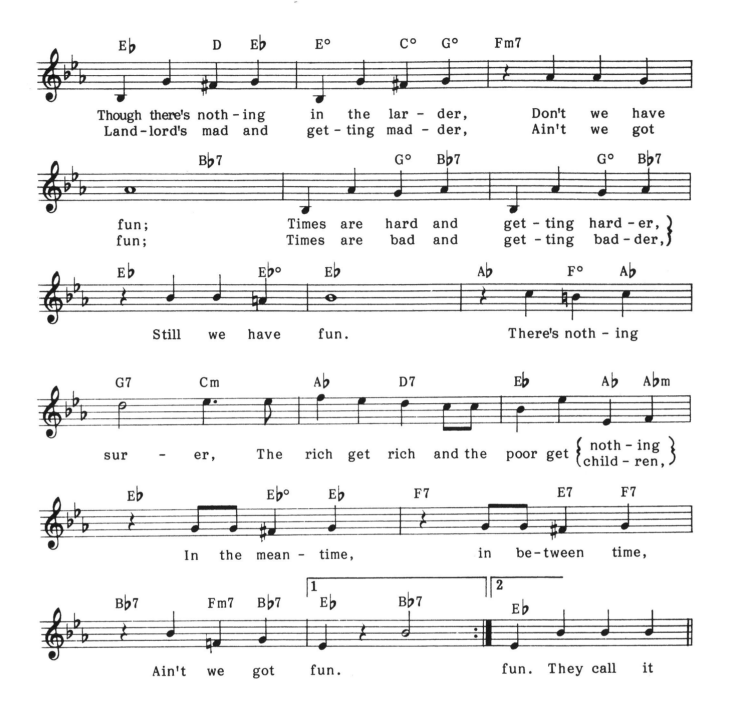

## BLACK BOTTOM

Words and Music by De SYLVA, BROWN and HENDERSON

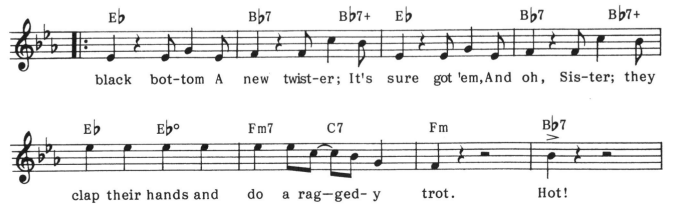

# THE CHARLESTON

Words & Music by CECIL MACK & JIMMY JOHNSON

Warner Chappell Music Ltd., London W1Y 3FA/Redwood Music Ltd., London NW1 8BD

# Medley 14 - Samba

## CHORANDO SE FOI
## (LAMBADA)

Words and Music by ULISES HERMOSA and GONZALO HERMOSA

Chor - an-do se foi

quem um di - a só me fez chor - ar, Chor - an-do se foi

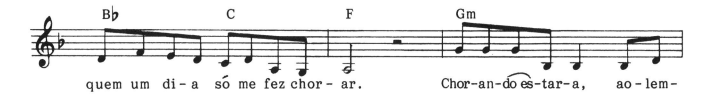

quem um di - a só me fez chor - ar. Chor-an-do es-tar-a, ao -lem-

brar de um a-mor que um di - a não soub-e cui - dar.

Chor-an-do es-tar-a, ao -lem - brar de um a-mor que um

di - a— não soub-e — cui - dar.—

## SAY SI SI

Words by AL STILLMAN and FRANCIA LUBAN
Music by ERNESTO LECUONA

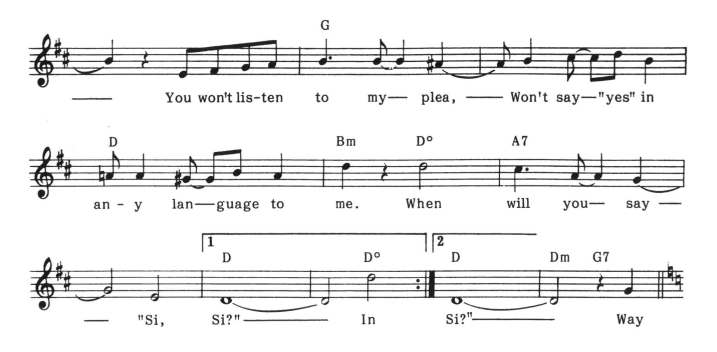

## THE COFFEE SONG

Words and Music by BOB HILLIARD and DICK MILES

## HAVA NAGILA

Traditional

# Medley 15 - Beguine

## BEGIN THE BEGUINE

Words and Music by COLE PORTER

When they be-gin ———

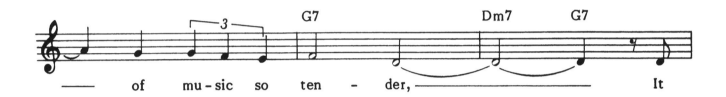

——— the be-guine, ——— It brings back the sound ———

——— of mu-sic so ten - der, ——— It

brings back a night ——— of tro-pic-al splen - dour, ———

——— It brings back a mem ——— or-y ev - er

green. ——— I'm with you once more ——— un-der the

stars ——— And down by the shore ———

an or–ches–tra's play – ing,——— And

e–ven the palms ——— seem to be sway – ing ———

When they be–gin ——— the be – guine. ———

– guine.

## Ay Ay Ay

Traditional

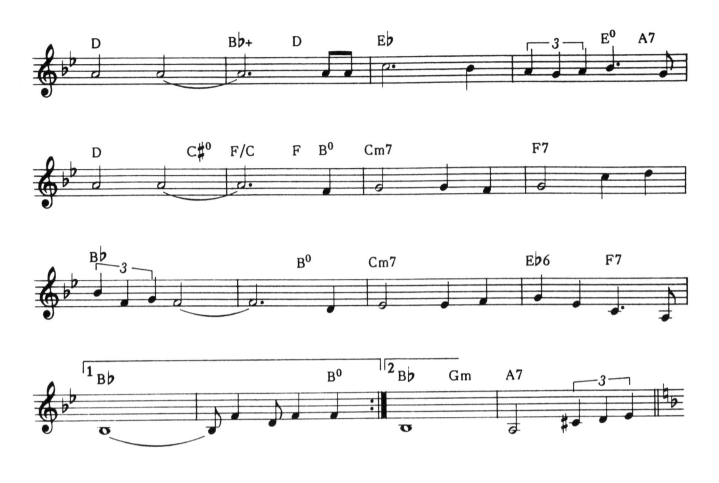

## BESAME MUCHO

English Lyrics by SUNNY SKYLAR
Music and Spanish Lyrics by CONSUELO VELAZQUEZ

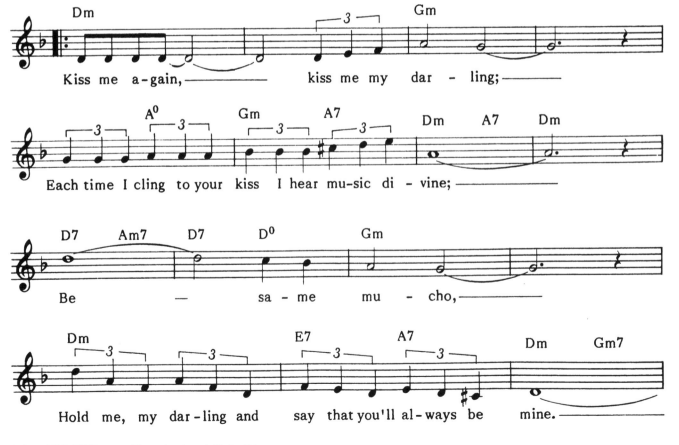

# Medley 16 - Cha Cha

**LA BAMBA**

RITCHIE VALENS

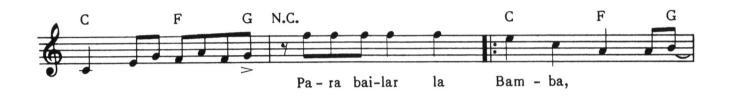

Pa - ra bai-lar la Bam - ba,

Pa-ra bai-lar la Bam-ba se ne - ce-si——ta una po-ca de

gra - cia, Un-a po-ca de gra-cia para mi pa-ra—

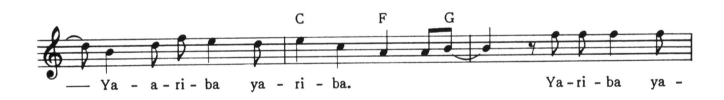

—Ya - a-ri-ba ya - ri - ba. Ya-ri-ba ya-

-ri-ba. Por ti - se - re,—— por ti se - re, por ti - se-re.—

—Yo no soy mar - i - ne - ro Yo no soy mar - i -

© 1958 & 1992 Kemo Music Company
Carlin Music Corporation, London NW1 8BD

- ne - ro. Soy cap - i -tan, —— soy cap - i - tan, soy cap - i -tan.——

—— Bam - ba, Bam —— ba, Bam - ba, Bam—

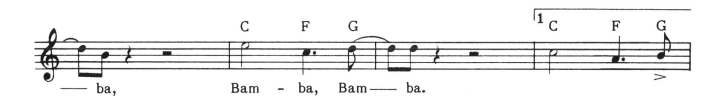

—— ba, Bam - ba, Bam —— ba.

Pa - ra-bai-lar la

## PATRICIA

Words by BOB MARCUS
Music by PEREZ PRADO

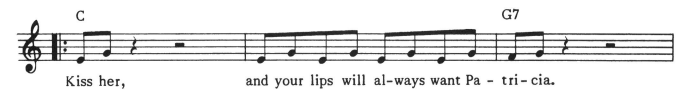

Kiss her, and your lips will al-ways want Pa - tri - cia.

Stroll her, see Pa -tri - cia move with all her

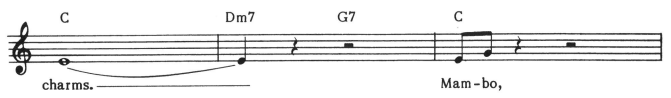

charms. —————————— Mam - bo,

cha cha or me-ren-gue, it's Pa - tri-cia.

Hea-ven, that's where you'll be when she's in your arms.

Who took the place of De De Di-nah? Pa-tri-cia! And Peg-gy Sue is jea-lous

too, of Pa-tri-cia. And when she's wearing her bi - ki - ni,

Her lips will have you hyp-no - tized.

Far off in Ja-pan, they brag a-bout their Gei-sha,

Who cares, 'long as Un-cle Sam has got Pa -

- tri-cia.                    - tri-cia.

# GUANTANAMERA

Traditional

# Medley 17 - Tango

## LA GOLONDRINA

Traditional

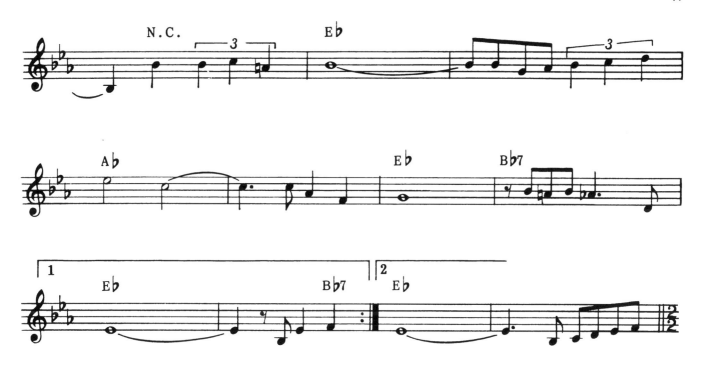

# I, YI, YI, YI, YI (I LIKE YOU VERY MUCH)

Words by MACK GORDON
Music by HARRY WARREN

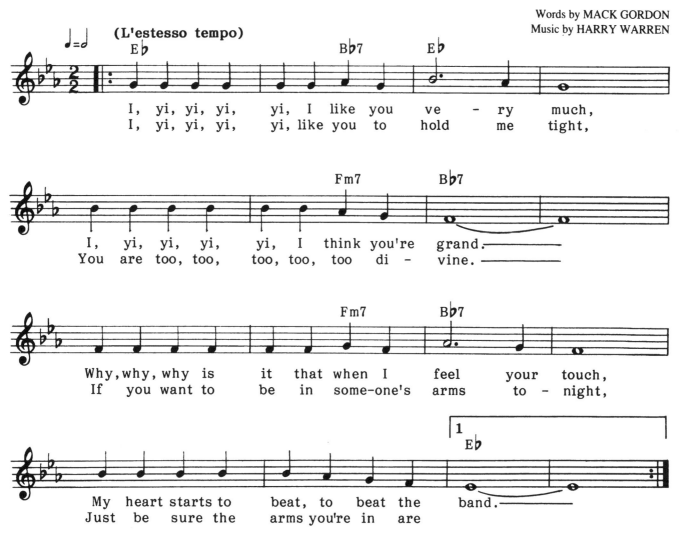

# O SOLE MIO

Traditional

Printed and bound in Great Britain by Caligraving Limited